What Santa Sees was written and produced as a planetarium show
by the team at the Life Science Centre in Newcastle upon Tyne, UK.
It was first shown in November 2023 and quickly became a sell-out success.
The show has since been bought by science centres
and planetarium domes across the world.

First edition published October 2024

Edited by Ben Rutherford-Orrock

ISBN 978-1-0685502-0-1

www.life.org.uk

WHAT
SANTA SEES

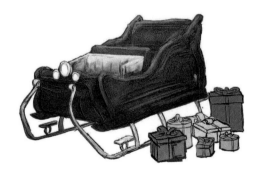

The sky's inky dark, the stars all aglow,
The moonlight is crisp on the fresh fallen snow.
There's a nip in the air, the breeze starts to blow,
Carrying jingling bells and a faint "Ho Ho Ho..."

It's Santa! He's busy preparing the sleigh,
Stacking the presents, sorting the hay,
Feeding the reindeer for the journey ahead,
As they circle the world whilst you lay in your bed.

Santa's sparkling eyes flicker here, flutter there,
As the Moon highlights tufts of his snowy white hair,
Casting shadows that dance and skip in a race,
His attention is caught by the Moon's shining face.

Some patches are darker, some look really bright,
The Moon is reflecting the hidden Sun's light.

The Sun is still there, though it cannot be found,
As the round Earth itself hides our star with the ground.

The spin of the Earth gives us night and then day,
As the Sun arcs around, the Moon lights the way.
The stars, Moon and planets give us quite the view,
As the evening draws deeper, more stars pierce through.

It's wintertime, days are short, nights are long.
We fill those dark evenings with stories and song.
Stars capture those stories, the sky's like a book,
Find dot-to-dot pictures, please come, take a look!

There's a dragon, a king, and a queen on her throne,
There's a little bear and a bear fully grown.
Watch as time passes and know that it's true,
Some stars twinkle red and some twinkle blue.

But carry on watching, the stars seem to spin,
And one star stays put, like it's stuck with a pin.
This one's Polaris, the star of the North,
With this star at his back, Santa's journey sets forth.

He's travelling south, with a sleigh full of treasure
Sprinkling hearts full of joy you can't measure,
Scattering cheer, making smiles, bringing merry,
With a belly of mince pies and the odd sip of sherry.

To the south! To New Zealand, Australia, Samoa.
With the curve of the Earth, Polaris dips lower.

New stars from the distant horizon rise up,
The majestic Orion, and Canis, his pup.

As they carry on south, Orion lifts high,
Then the dog and Orion cross over the sky.
The stars in this pattern now look all switched round.
This giant hunter is now upside down!

Bright pinpoints of light that shine in the dark,
Every once in a while there streaks a bright spark.
A flash through the night, a shooting star, bright!
Santa closes his eyes, makes a wish at the sight.

Into our atmosphere, tumbling down,
A rock glows so brightly it lights up the town.
This shooting star's just a small grain of dust,
Santa sees it, but carry on going he must.

Before him, eager children are failing to settle,
Their excitement boils over, like water in a kettle.

Behind him, shrieks of joy as they rise,
And children find stockings stuffed full of surprise.

These memories made are not witnessed by Santa,
Or the soft-footed reindeer as onwards they canter.
They must keep on racing to carry on winning,
Their deadline can't wait, as the Earth keeps on spinning.

From the east to the west, Santa travels the globe,
Sometimes warmer or colder, adjusting his robe.
Leaving presents behind, Santa empties his sack,
Then he moves on again, keeping dawn at his back.

With so many places to see on their flight,
It's almost too much to do in one night;
Beijing, Bangkok, Kabul, and Cairo,
Kinshasa, Newcastle, Caracas, San Diego.

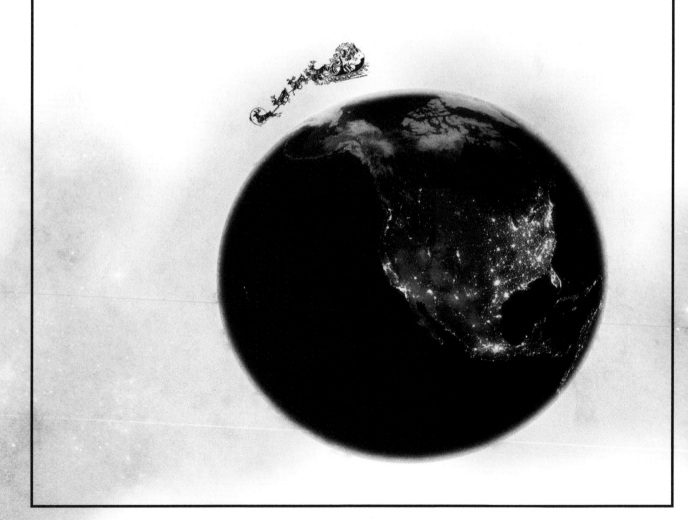

Tired and confused as he reaches the end,
Santa's not sure where the reindeer to send.
His parcels are gone, he feels all alone,
He no longer remembers the way back to home.

"Is this the way north?" He says with a sigh,
Then looks up and sees some old friends in the sky.
The big bear and little bear show him the way,
And it seems that to Santa, together they say...

"Look out for the star of the north in the sky,
Keep heading towards it and watch it rise high.
When Polaris is at the very top of the dome,
You'll know that it signals you're finally home."

So the reindeer and Santa head back to the snow,
Though his sleigh is now empty, his heart's all aglow.
The sky up above fills with curtains of light,
With colours that make Santa gasp at the sight.

His job is complete for the full year ahead,
And Santa can hear the sweet call of his bed.
But first, to the stables, to tuck in his reindeer,
Removing their saddles and all of their sleigh-gear.

Giving each a warm blanket, and a pat on their nose,
As together they huddle, beginning to doze.
As children all over shout "Santa's the best!"
Santa's head hits the pillow to finally rest.

THE END

BV - #0030 - 301024 - C32 - 210/210/2 - PB - 9781068550201 - Gloss Lamination